If the Bible really is "  than gold",
"sweeter than honey", then we want to do everything
we can to get hold of it. And, moreover, to let it get
hold of us. Richard Chin is a man who loves God's
word and has allowed it to shape him over a lifetime of ministry.
In this short and sweet book, let him help you treasure
God's word as you read it and apply it.

Ben Carswell
National Director, TSCF, New Zealand

Richard Chin has written a great guide to reading the
Bible. Is that something you've thought of doing this
year? Reading this very short book will help you read
that longer book—the Bible—better. In this book you'll
find simple, direct help, short and useful, sane, clear,
and basic. So much wisdom packed into so few pages!
Chin has been reading his Bible for a long time, and
can help us do it, too.

Mark Dever
Pastor, Capitol Hill Baptist Church, Washington DC
President, 9Marks.org

One of the most pressing needs we face as evangeli-
cals in Australia today is to read our Bibles more and
better. Richard has given us a brilliant resource (which
is both a shot in the arm and a kick in the pants!) to
throw ourselves into grappling with what God has
said to us in his word with fresh energy and focus.

Gary Millar
Principal, Queensland Theological College
Co-author, *Saving Eutychus*

Richard's writing is always wonderfully clear and straightforward, and this work is no exception. This is a great resource to put into the hands of disciplers, new Christians, and, really, any church member looking to grow in the faith. Here is a short book to help us read The Book even better.

Kevin DeYoung
Senior Pastor, Christ Covenant Church, Matthews, NC

Reading and living in the light of the written word that God has given is both a challenge and an enormous privilege. All sorts of pressures are trying to fix our attention elsewhere. Yet it is the word of God that shapes lives and builds churches. Richard Chin's little book will encourage you to read and teach the Bible, to listen attentively to these words God has given us, to delight in the Bible as well as to bend every effort to live it to the full. If the Bible seems a strange and threatening word to you, buy this book and be encouraged. If you are tempted to set aside the Bible in order to speak the words our neighbours want to hear and in the tone in which they want to hear them, buy this book and stand firm at this point. If you want to be reminded why the ministry of the word of God is the most important work there is in the world, buy this book and recapture the vision of life lived with and under the word of the living God.

Mark D Thompson
Principal, Moore Theological College, Sydney

Richard Chin packs everything you want in a book about the Bible into this small, accessible volume. This book isn't just a how-to manual for sound interpretation (though it is that!); it's also a glorious meditation on the worth of God's word, an encouragement to humble our hearts before God, and an invitation to see how Jesus fulfils God's promises and how every passage of Scripture unfolds the gospel of our Lord. If you love the Bible, you should get this book. If you love to teach others how to read the Bible better, you should buy multiple copies and give them away.

Sam Emadi
Senior Editor, 9Marks.org

Store up this gem of a book in your spiritual treasure chest! Richard Chin has written a delightful book filled with insight about reading the word of God. Don't let the brevity fool you—it's deep, clever, and fun. In a world that increasingly uses the Bible poorly, every Christian should read this book. It is so full of scriptural insight that, as I read, I found myself not just learning how to read the Bible better, but worshipping the one who gave us the Bible.

Mack Stiles
Pastor, Erbil International Baptist Church, Iraq
Author, *Marks of the Messenger*

The apostle Peter urges his readers, "like newborn babies, crave the wordy milk so that you may grow up in your salvation". This outstanding book not only helps us to read and understand the Bible better; it also left me longing to study it more. It covers complex material with characteristic clarity and winsome appeal. There are so many good lessons well taught. Reading the book and putting it into practice will leave us craving God's word and growing to maturity. I wholeheartedly recommend it.

William Taylor
Rector, St Helen's Bishopsgate, London

This little book contains many big ideas that are massively important. It shows us how and why we should read the Bible so that we meet God and hear him speak. Richard has distilled his vast experience and wisdom as a Bible reader and Bible teacher into a book that will equip you to more faithfully and fruitfully read the Bible yourself and with others.

David Walter
South Pacific Regional Secretary, IFES

HOW TO READ
THE BIBLE
BETTER

RICHARD CHIN

matthiasmedia
SYDNEY · YOUNGSTOWN

Matthias Media
(St Matthias Press Ltd ACN 067 558 365)
Email: info@matthiasmedia.com.au
Internet: www.matthiasmedia.com.au
Please visit our website for current postal and telephone contact information.

Matthias Media (USA)
Email: sales@matthiasmedia.com
Internet: www.matthiasmedia.com
Please visit our website for current postal and telephone contact information.

ISBN 978 1 875245 83 3

Cover design and typesetting by Lankshear Design.

CONTENTS

Introduction   5

1. Why read the Bible?   9

2. How do I read the Bible better?   17

3. A framework for better Bible reading   21

4. The treasures are *in the text*   29

5. A text without a context is a con   39

6. Let Scripture interpret Scripture   47

Conclusion: The joy of your heart   57

Appendix: A word for those privileged
to teach others   59

INTRODUCTION

Have you ever found the Bible difficult to read? You sit down with your tea and notebook, eager to hear God speak, but the words seem foreign and distant. What's an 'Asherah'? Who are the 'Amalekites'? How do I even pronounce 'Abiezrites'?[1]

It might be tempting to search for something relevant by randomly dipping into the Bible. John Stott tells the story of what it's like for the man who tries this method. He closes his eyes, flicks through the pages, and points blindly to Matthew 27:5: "He [Judas] went and hanged himself". Understandably dismayed, the man tries flicking again, only to land on Luke 10:37: "You go, and do likewise". So he tries one more time and finds John 13:27: "What you are

1   These words all appear in Judges 6.

going to do, do quickly".[2] Not exactly what he had hoped for!

Many people have opened the pages of Scripture eager to feast on the word of God, only to end up feeling failed and deflated. But persevere, dear friend. Nothing is more life-giving than God's word (Ps 119:25). Nothing is more desirable than God's word (Ps 19:10). Nothing is more deadly than starvation from God's word (Amos 8:11). Nothing is more deceiving than God's word distorted (Gen 3:1-5; 2 Pet 3:16).

Rosaria Butterfield straddled two lives for two years: one as a lesbian lover, and the other as a regular Bible reader. This is her story:

> After years and years… something
> happened. The Bible got to be bigger inside
> me than I. It overflowed into my world. And
> then one Sunday morning… two years after
> I started reading the Bible for my research,
> I left the bed I shared with my lesbian
> partner and an hour later I showed up in a
> pew at the Syracuse Reformed Presbyterian
> Church… I kept going back to church to hear
> more sermons. I had made friendships with

2   J Stott, *Students of the Word*, IFES, 2013, p. 34.

people in the church by this time and I had
really appreciated the way that they talked
about the sermons throughout the week, how
the word of God dwelt in them, and how they
referenced it in the details of their days.[3]

It's a glorious picture of God transforming Rosaria through his powerful word: the Bible "got to be bigger inside [her]"! But did you also see the beautiful image of church members nurturing one another with the word? Teachers of God's word have a particular God-given responsibility in the church.[4] But the ministry of God's word is the privilege of *every* brother and sister in Christ. When the apostle Paul wrote "Let the word of Christ dwell in you richly, teaching and admonishing *one another* in all wisdom" (Col 3:16), it was his instruction to *every* member of the Colossian church.[5] The apostle's desire was for believers to consider how to stir up *one another* and encourage *one another* from the Scriptures as they saw the Day of Christ's return drawing near (cf. Heb 10:24-25). Isn't this what we long for? This is a key reason we want to read the

3   R Butterfield, *Openness Unhindered*, Crown & Covenant, 2015, p. 22 (emphasis added).
4   See 1 Timothy 3:1-7, 5:17; Titus 1:5-9.
5   I have added any emphasis that appears in Bible passages throughout this book.

Bible better: not just to grow our own understanding of God and our trust in him, but to help others do likewise, so that every preacher, pew sitter and pauper might rise from death to life and help *one another* along this narrow path as we journey to the glory-land together.[6]

But this is not just a book for Christians. If you've picked up this book as someone who doesn't yet follow Jesus, my prayer is that these brief pages will help you delight in hearing the voice of your Creator *in the Bible*. He desires all people, including you, to be saved and to come to the knowledge of the truth (1 Tim 2:4). I hope learning why and how to read the Bible will help you find the saving knowledge it conveys.

---

6   By 'better', I mean reading God's word the way he intended it to be read, on his terms, for his church, for his world, supremely for his glory. As such, the Bible is not just a private charter for his church; "[the Bible] is a total claim on the whole world. God, the creator, owner, and governor of the world, has spoken. His words are valid and binding on all people everywhere. That is what it means to be God" (J Piper, *Reading the Bible Supernaturally: Seeing and Savoring the Glory of God in Scripture*, Crossway, p. 33).

1.
WHY READ THE BIBLE?

How do I read the Bible so that, as Rosaria Butterfield said, it "overflow[s] into my world"? Listening to sermons is (relatively) easy, and songs can lift the soul... but the Bible? Why read it? Is it really worth the effort? Here are seven reasons to get you started.

1. The Bible is God's revelation of himself

God isn't hidden. He has spoken. The Lord of heaven and earth "forfeited his own personal privacy" to disclose himself to us—to befriend us—through a book.[7] Scripture is like an all-access pass into the revealed mind and will of God.

7   CFH Henry, *God, Revelation and Authority,* vol. II, *God Who Speaks and Shows,* Crossway, 1999, quoted in M Smethurst, '8 Things Your Bible Says About Itself', *The Gospel Coalition,* US edition, 29 July 2020. thegospelcoalition.org/article/bible-says-about-itself

Although the divine glory of God is magnificently seen in the natural world (e.g. Psalm 19; Rom 1:18-20), it is supremely seen in the person of Jesus Christ: "the Word became flesh and dwelt among us, and we have seen his glory, glory as of the only Son from the Father, full of grace and truth" (John 1:14). The Old Testament Scriptures bear witness about Jesus (John 5:39), as do the New Testament Scriptures. What the apostles saw face-to-face in Jesus Christ, they impart to us through the words of Scripture (1 John 1:3). The glory they saw in Christ, we can see through their words in the Bible.[8]

2. The Bible is exposing

As we read the Scriptures, God exposes us. He cuts through our disguises to discern all "the thoughts and intentions of the heart" (Heb 4:12). Through the Bible, the Holy Spirit convicts the world concerning sin and righteousness and judgement (John 16:8-11), so that the Bible uncovers our sin as we read it. Even though this can make Bible reading awkward or even painful on occasion, we come to know our true self. What a gracious act of God!

8   Piper, *Reading the Bible Supernaturally*, p. 22.

3. The Bible is life-giving

When God put Ezekiel in the middle of the valley full of dry bones, he said, "Prophesy over these bones, and say to them, O dry bones, hear the word of the LORD. Thus says the Lord GOD to these bones: Behold, I will cause breath to enter you, and you shall live" (Ezek 37:4-5). When God commands Ezekiel to prophesy God's word over the dead bones, God breathes life into them!

So the psalmist writes: "I will never forget your precepts, for by them you have given me life" (Ps 119:93). We too can only find life in the Scriptures. As the disciples knew, only Jesus has "the words of eternal life" (John 6:68).

4. The Bible is profitable

"All Scripture is breathed out by God and profitable for teaching, for reproof, for correction, and for training in righteousness, that the man of God may be complete, equipped for every good work" (2 Tim 3:16-17).

As we've seen already, God's word can rebuke and correct us, but here we see it also trains us to live righteously.

Do also note that God "breathed out" the words of Scripture himself. Just as our breath carries our words, so God's breath carries his words from within his heart, from inside himself, to the pages of Scripture. Thus, what can be said about God can be said about his word. The way we treat God's word is the way we treat God. How we think and feel about God matches precisely with how we think and feel about his word. That's why the Bible will profitably teach us, rebuke us, correct us, and train us in righteousness.[9]

5. The Bible is our only offensive weapon

As we journey towards Christ's coming kingdom, we're at war. Our ultimate battle is not against flesh and blood, but against "the spiritual forces of evil in the heavenly places" (Eph 6:12). By God's grace, he has already won the war by triumphing over the cosmic rulers and authorities at the cross of Christ (Col 2:13-15). Satan is irreversibly defeated. And yet, even as our has-been-defeated enemy, he still

9   Many argue (I think rightly) that the term 'man of God' in 2 Timothy 3:17 refers to those in ministry leadership like Timothy. In the Old Testament, the phrase 'man of God' is used of Moses (Deut 33:1; Psalm 90), angelic beings (Judg 13:6; 1 Sam 2:27), Samuel (1 Sam 9:6 ff.), Elijah (1 Kgs 17:18), Elisha (2 Kgs 4:7), and David (Neh 12:24). In the New Testament, the phrase 'man of God' is *only* used of Timothy, in 1 Timothy 6:11. So the Scriptures are particularly apt to train God's *leaders* for every good work. But, by implication, they will do likewise for *all Christians*.

wages a counteroffensive until Christ returns for final judgement (Revelation 12).

Abraham Kuyper describes this battle as follows:

> If once the curtain were pulled back, and the spiritual world behind it came to view, it would expose to our spiritual vision a struggle so intense, so convulsive, sweeping everything within its range, that the fiercest battle fought on earth would seem, by comparison, a mere game.[10]

It is in this context that God has graciously given us spiritual armour for protection. God protects us with the armour of truth, righteousness, peace, faith and salvation. But the only offensive weapon needed in our armoury is "the sword of the Spirit, which is the word of God" (Eph 6:10-20). Just as Christ fought against the flaming arrows of Satan's temptations with the Scriptures (Matt 4:1-11), so too we fight with our only offensive weapon, the word of God.

10 Quoted in C Brauns, 'Remember, We're In A War', *Chris Brauns' blog,* September 2008. chrisbrauns.com/2008/09/remember-were-in-a-war

6. The Bible is our supreme authority in living life for God and his glory

I say 'supreme' because there are other authorities we ought to acknowledge. The diagram below shows a useful 'authority quadrilateral' derived from the ministry of John Wesley.[11]

Bible	Reason
Tradition	Experience

It is impossible to read the Bible without using your reason, or your experience, and it is always helpful to learn from historical traditions. The question is, which authority will you choose when any of these other authorities conflicts with Scripture? For example, some Christian denominations have chosen to approve same-sex unions by choosing the authority of reason and experience over the plain meaning of Scripture, which clearly teaches that God has designed marriage to be an unbreakable bond between one man and one woman for life.

11 'Wesleyan Quadrilateral' in *Theopedia*. theopedia.com/wesleyan-quadrilateral

Similarly, other denominations choose to pray to other 'saints' as well as to God because they have chosen the authority of church tradition over the plain meaning of Scripture. But we mustn't be deluded by "plausible arguments" (Col 2:4). The word of God is "a lamp to [our] feet and a light to [our] path" (Ps 119:105). Scripture is the supreme authority in all matters of life and conduct.

7. The Bible is sufficient for all that we need to know about God and how to live for him

When life gets confusing, or really tough, we do not need more revelation from God outside of the Bible to navigate these times. The Bible has *all* the principles we need to make any decision in life. JI Packer writes:

> Scripture provides clear and exact guidance for every detail and department of life, and if we come to Scripture teachably and expectantly God himself will seal on our minds and hearts a clear certainty as to how we should behave in each situation that faces us.[12]

12   JI Packer, *A Quest For Godliness: The Puritan Vision of the Christian Life*, Crossway, 1994, p. 113.

So why read the Bible?

I love the way John Owen says it:

> Scripture is given to make us humble, holy,
> wise in spiritual things; to direct us in our
> duties, to relieve us in our temptations, to
> comfort us under troubles, to make us to
> love God and to live unto him... Unto this
> end there is a more glorious power and
> efficacy in one epistle, one Psalm, one
> chapter, than in all the writings of men.[13]

Small wonder that the psalmist can describe God's word as "more to be desired... than gold" and "sweeter also than honey and drippings of the honeycomb" (Ps 19:10).

13   John Owen, *The Works of John Owen,* vol. IV, *The Work of the
     Holy Spirit,* Banner of Truth, 1967, pp. 188-90.

2.
HOW DO I READ THE BIBLE BETTER?

Perhaps you're expecting this chapter to be a how-to guide, with practical instructions. Don't worry, we will get there. But first, better Bible reading means approaching the Bible...

1. Supernaturally

The Bible requires more than your natural reading. Not less. But more. It calls for the best of your natural reading. But it also calls for more because it is breathed out by God (2 Tim 3:16).[14] Reading the Bible is not a mundane experience. You are encountering

---

14   cf. Piper, *Reading the Bible Supernaturally,* p. 19.

the voice of the living God. Reading the Bible is the most supernatural experience of the Christian life.

2. Prayerfully

Like the psalmist, we can pray: "Open my eyes, that I may behold wondrous things out of your law" (Ps 119:18), or "Incline my heart to your testimonies, and not to selfish gain!" (Ps 119:36). Indeed, prayer is an essential element of good Bible reading, for it is only when God illuminates his word that we can understand it and trust it. "The natural person does not accept the things of the Spirit of God, for they are folly to him, and he is not able to understand them because they are spiritually discerned" (1 Cor 2:14).

3. Meditatively

"Make me understand the way of your precepts, and I will *meditate* on your wondrous works" (Ps 119:27). It's one thing to read the Bible, but it is another thing to *meditate* on it. Meditation definitely does not mean reading the Bible for a few minutes, then switching off your mind and seeking some trance-like state of 'heightened spiritual awareness'. It's quite the opposite. In Christianity, meditation means engaging your mind more fully.

It means thinking deeply on what the Bible says and on how we should apply it over and over again.

4. Obediently

"I have stored up your word in my heart, that I might not sin against you" (Ps 119:11). One way to store up God's word is to memorize it, not purely to gain knowledge, but to love (1 Cor 8:1). And *the* way to love Jesus is to obey his commandments contained in Scripture (John 14:15).

5. Eternally

"For whatever was written in former days was written for our instruction, that through endurance and through the encouragement of the Scriptures we might have hope" (Rom 15:4). God wrote the Bible for us who stand on the precipice of eternity to encourage us to look forward with purpose in Christ-exalting hope.

6. Delightfully

Just as we can delight in and long for God, so too we can delight in and long for his word.

"I will delight in your statutes; I will not forget your word" (Ps 119:16). "My soul is consumed

with longing for your just decrees at all times"
(Ps 119:20).[15]

7. With trembling

"But this is the one to whom I will look: he who is humble and contrite in spirit and trembles at my word" (Isa 66:2). Reading the Bible is not a casual activity. We are to treat God's word like we treat God, and that means trembling.

Delight and trembling are a strange mix of emotions. But we need both! Trembling without delight can dissolve into a blind and inappropriate terror. But a delight without trembling easily dissolves into a superficial piety without a real passion for holiness. Reading the Bible will require both for the glory of God.

15 See also Psalm 119:35, 47, 70, 77, 92, 143, 162, 174.

3.
A FRAMEWORK FOR BETTER BIBLE READING[16]

In utter dependence upon God, how then do we inform our minds and hearts to read the Bible better?

In this chapter we'll work through the following framework, clause by clause:

> **The Bible was written by God,**
> **through people, to others, about Jesus,**
> **for us on the edge of eternity.**

---

16   I am indebted to David Walter for this framework, which he presented at the AFES National Training Event in 2019; see 'NTE19 Talk 5: Encountering God's Spirit', *NTE19: Encountering God*, AFES website, 12 December 2019. afes.org.au/talks/nte19-talk-5-encountering-gods-spirit

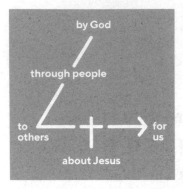

by God

through people

to others

about Jesus

for us

1. The Bible was written *by God*

Our good, gracious and holy God is the ultimate author of the Bible. As the author, *he* establishes the meaning of the Scriptures. He says what he means, and what he says is always good.[17]

Although this sounds obvious, there is a growing tendency in academic circles to say that a text means what the *reader* determines, and not what the *author* intended.[18] In this understanding, what a text means to me may be different to what it means to you. That makes the Bible infinitely interpretable. But it is not! The Bible means only what our good God intended it to mean. Our delight as Bible readers is *not to interpret* the Bible on *our* terms, but to prayerfully *comprehend* what

---

17 The ploy of the serpent in Genesis 3 was to make Adam and Eve doubt the goodness of God by doubting the goodness of his word.

18 As an English Professor, Rosaria Butterfield used to teach her students that "a text's meaning found its power only in the reader's interpretation of it... without the reader, a book is just paper and glue"; see *Openness Unhindered*, p. 21. The great irony, of course, is that those who hold this view commonly use *texts* to articulate it (with every expectation that readers will understand their message).

God means on *his* terms, so that we can lovingly obey him.

2. The Bible was written by God *through people*

God is the ultimate author of his word. As Peter says, "no prophecy of Scripture comes from someone's own interpretation. For no prophecy was ever produced by the will of man, but men spoke from God as they were carried along by the Holy Spirit" (2 Pet 1:20-21). Yet God chose *human authors* to write Scripture, who wrote with their own personalities and writing styles. Ezekiel does not sound the same as Isaiah, who does not sound the same as Jeremiah; Peter does not write like Paul, who does not write like John.

3. The Bible was written by God through people *to others*

Each of the human authors of the Bible wrote to *specific* people or specific churches at specific times and places. They did not write *directly* to us. The Old Testament authors wrote primarily to the people of Israel, while Paul wrote to specific churches in places like Thessalonica and Rome and to specific individuals like Timothy and Titus.

4. The Bible was written by God through people to others *about Jesus*

After Jesus rose from the dead, he appeared to his disciples and said, "everything written *about me* in the Law of Moses and the Prophets and the Psalms must be fulfilled" (Luke 24:44). Jesus is saying that the right way to understand the Old Testament is to see how it is ultimately fulfilled *in him*. Likewise, Peter makes this astonishing point by attributing the words of the Old Testament to the Spirit of Christ: "the prophets who prophesied about the grace that was to be yours searched and inquired carefully, inquiring what person or time the Spirit of Christ in them was indicating when he predicted the sufferings of Christ and the subsequent glories" (1 Pet 1:10-11).

So if the Spirit-inspired Old Testament points to Jesus, what about the New Testament? After all, it wasn't written when Jesus walked this earth. But Jesus authorized the New Testament writings by equipping his apostles with his Spirit (just as he did the Old Testament prophets): "the Helper, the Holy Spirit, whom the Father will send in my name, he will teach you all things and bring to your remembrance all that I have said to you" (John 14:26). As such, these New Testament authors spoke from

God as they were carried along by the Holy Spirit. So it should be no surprise that they, too, write ultimately about our Lord Jesus Christ—the one to whom the Holy Spirit consistently points.[19]

To read the Bible better, we must see how Jesus gets centre stage.

5. The Bible was written by God through people to others about Jesus *for us*

Even though the Bible was not written directly *to* us, we have the amazing privilege of knowing that it has all been written *for* us. Again, speaking of the Old Testament prophets, Peter writes: "It was revealed to them that they were serving *not themselves but you*, in the things that have *now been announced to you* through those who preached the good news to you by the Holy Spirit sent from heaven, things into which angels long to look" (1 Pet 1:12). Referring to the account of Israel in the books of Exodus and Numbers, Paul writes: "these things took place as examples *for us*, that we may not desire evil as they did" (1 Cor 10:6).

---

19 We'll say more about this when we look at biblical theology in chapter 6.

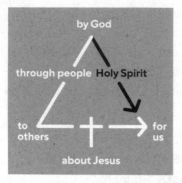

But, you might think, surely God can speak directly to us by his Spirit today (like the black arrow in the diagram). Surely this is more miraculous than the laborious framework in the Bible. It's true! God *can* speak directly to us apart from the Bible *if he chooses*. But he does not *promise* to speak directly to us like this. God chose to speak directly to Balaam through a donkey in Numbers 22, but he never promised to keep doing so. Likewise, God spoke directly to King Belshazzar by writing on a wall in Daniel 5. But my guess is that you don't expect God to speak to you today through donkeys or graffiti, because he doesn't promise to do so, even though he can!

As the author of Hebrews says, "Long ago, at *many times* and in *many ways* [such as donkeys, writing on the wall, dreams and visions, to name a few], God spoke to our fathers by the prophets..." (Heb 1:1). But he doesn't promise to keep doing so. What he does promise is to speak to us *by*, and *about*, his Son: "...but in these last days he has spoken to us by his Son" (Heb 1:2).

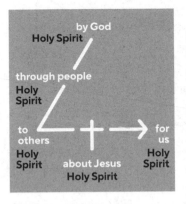

In fact, as the diagram shows, it is as if the Holy Spirit is at work five times more through the process of speaking to us in the Bible than if he were to speak directly to us. So, if you're looking for the most spiritual approach, you can't get more spiritual than reading the Bible better!

And if we are to read the Bible better, we will need to work hard to understand how it is ultimately written by God, through people, to others about Jesus... for us.

6. The Bible was written by God, through people, to others, about Jesus, for us *on the edge of eternity*

As Bible readers *today*, we live on the edge of eternity.[20]

---

20 Theologians often call this area of study 'eschatology', which is the study of the last things. This refers (among other things) to the return of Jesus and the events that come before and after, which affect us in the here and now. Eschatology helps us to read the Bible better because it applies Scripture properly by placing us on the precipice of eternity. From this vantage point, we look forward with hope and purpose.

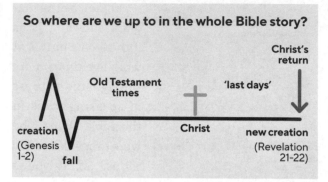

So where are we up to in the whole Bible story?

Christ's return

Old Testament times

'last days'

creation (Genesis 1-2)

fall

Christ

new creation (Revelation 21-22)

We live in the 'last days' with the certain hope of a new creation, and can consider our present sufferings as incomparable with the glory that will be revealed to us (Rom 8:18-25). On the one hand, we live in the same times of difficulty that Paul and Timothy lived in, where people lived as lovers of self rather than lovers of God (2 Tim 3:1-4). Like the Thessalonians, we live as those who wait for Christ's return (1 Thess 1:10). And our lives must be shaped by the knowledge that the end of all things is at hand (1 Pet 4:7-11). Knowing our eternal setting will help us read the Bible better.

Understanding the Bible with this framework will require the best of our natural reading—and more. For ultimately, we can only read the Bible better in supernatural dependence upon God.

4.
THE TREASURES ARE
IN THE TEXT

Often, the Bible resonates strongly with our feelings and experiences. This can be comforting when reading verses like "God is love" (1 John 4:8). But how do you feel when you read that "[we] were by nature children of wrath, like the rest of mankind" (Eph 2:3)?

How are we to 'interpret' such verses?

One way is to insert our preferred meaning into the text. For example, some people might say that Ephesians 2:3 doesn't speak of God's anger, but refers simply to the "inevitable process of cause and effect in a moral Universe."[21] The technical

---

21   John Stott refers to such academics in *The Cross of Christ*, IVP, Leicester, 1986, pp. 103-4.

term for this is 'eisegesis', which literally means 'consider *into*'—reading things *into* the text, rather than out of the text. Sadly, when this happens, we will:

a. miss out on what God *is* saying, and

b. falsely sanctify what God is *not* saying.

Instead, we need to *exegete* the Bible. 'Exegesis' literally means 'consider *out of*'. It is the activity of considering the meaning that comes out of the text; it is the opposite of 'eisegesis'. **Put simply, 'exegesis' is comprehending God's intended meaning out of the text.**

That's why it is better to speak of *comprehending* a text, rather than interpreting it. What people mean by interpretation today often involves inserting their preferred meaning into a text. This often arises from ignorant or accidental assumptions that the Bible is written directly to us (as we discussed in chapter 3). It can also arise when we are uncomfortable with the plain comprehension of a text that causes us to doubt God's goodness. References to God's anger, for example, have been fertile ground for reading more palatable meanings into the text (eisegesis) rather than plainly comprehending what comes out of the text (exegesis).

How, then, do we exegete better?

1. Make careful observations

As we approach the Bible (see chapter 2), our task is to find God's meaning by firstly reading the text with careful observation. A zoology student was once asked to study a specimen of a dead fish. "How easy!" he thought. After several minutes, he believed his task complete, but after repeated pushing by his professor to come up with more, the student eventually realized how many observations he had missed.[22] "You've barely begun!" the professor urged.

When it comes to the Bible, the treasures are in the text! Prayerfully see what you can discover as you read the passage over and over again, making careful observations.

2. Ask questions of the text, and then try and answer them out of the text

Ask the five Ws: who, what, where, when, why.

Every text will have an author, an audience, and a purpose for having been written. Work to discover these *from the text*.

---

22   'In the Laboratory with Agassiz', *Every Saturday: A journal of choice reading*, vol. I, no. 14, 4 April 1874, pp. 369-70. babel.hathitrust.org/cgi/pt?id=mdp.39015030073863

Every text will also have a structure. So note the flow and logic, or the progression of thought. How does the argument (in letters) or story (in narrative) evolve? How is it resolved? To discover the logic, look for any connecting words (especially in letters). For example, in Romans 3:21, Paul starts the sentence with "But now" to contrast the new way in which "the righteousness of God has been manifested" ("*apart* from the Law", through the death of Jesus) with the old way ("by works of the law"; 3:20). And this introduces what is probably the most significant paragraph in the Bible concerning the death of Jesus (Rom 3:21-26).

Look for repeated phrases or words. Repetition emphasizes something significant. Again, the phrase "righteousness of God" is repeated throughout Romans, referring to God's standards as Creator and Judge—a major theme in Romans.

What is the genre? The literary styles within the Bible include historical narrative (e.g. the Gospels or Acts), wisdom literature (e.g. Proverbs), poetry (e.g. Psalms), prophecy (e.g. Jeremiah), apocalyptic literature (e.g. Revelation), and letters or epistles (e.g. Romans). As with all literature, the genre changes how we read it. You would read a novel by Jane Austen quite differently to a recipe book by Nigella. The genre determines how you read the text.

If the text is a narrative (like Matthew), ask the question, "Is this a *descriptive* passage or a *prescriptive* passage?" For example, the apostles were sent out to heal the sick, raise the dead, cleanse lepers, and cast out demons (Matt 10:8). This *describes* their specific mission, but it does not *prescribe* what God intends for every believer. However, later in the same chapter, Jesus goes on to say: "*Whoever loves father and mother more than me is not worthy of me*" (v. 37 ff.). This is clearly a comment for every believer.

Here's another example: in Acts 2, the disciples are described as those who "began to speak in other tongues as the Spirit gave them utterance" (v. 4). In the context, this is later interpreted in verse 33: "Being therefore exalted at the right hand of God, and having received from the Father the promise of the Holy Spirit, he has poured out this that you yourselves are seeing and hearing". In other words, Acts 2 describes 'speaking in tongues' as a Spirit-empowered phenomenon that pointed to the exaltation of Jesus to God's right hand on that specific day. It does not prescribe what all believers should do today. Rather, the prescription for speaking in tongues comes in 1 Corinthians 14, where we read (among other things) that it is to be avoided unless it can be interpreted and weighed. God's word will always shape our minds, hearts and lives by giving us a clearer picture of who God is and how he has acted to save his people. But, just as in our example, this doesn't mean that every passage prescribes how we should act. Take the time to read each passage carefully so you can discern the difference.

If the text is poetry (like the psalms), look for lines that parallel each other to emphasize a point, or to contrast a point. For example, in Psalm 1:1 we read: "Blessed is the man who walks *not* in the counsel of the wicked, *nor* stands in the way of sinners, *nor* sits in the seat of scoffers".[23] Here the psalmist uses parallel ideas to emphasize different postures that describe how the wicked become more comfortable with sin. They walk, then stand, then sit. In Hebrew poetry, we would expect the psalmist to describe the opposite behaviour with the same parallels (what scholars call 'antithetical parallelism') in verse 2, which would look something like this: "Blessed is the one who walks in the counsel of the *righteous*, who stands in the way of the *godly*, and who sits in the seat of the *worshippers*". But instead, the psalmist says there

23 The singular Hebrew word for 'man' is used here of men and women who portray the life of a blessed person.

is only one thing needed for the blessed one: "his delight is in the law of the LORD, and on his law he *meditates* day and night". The radical rejection of wicked ideas, sinful behaviour, and scoffing speech occurs by joyfully meditating on God's word.[24] How important are the Scriptures!

What is clear? What is unclear? The book of Revelation is the prime example of apocalyptic literature. As such, it is full of symbols. In Revelation 4, the most repeated symbol is the 'throne', which is the seat of power and kingship that belongs to God. What is *unclear* to me at the time of writing is the exact identity of the four living creatures and the twenty-four elders. They could represent all the creatures of the world and the people of God, or orders of representative angels, or something else besides. But what is *clear* is what they are doing: they give all glory, honour and power to God *in heaven* because he created them all (v. 11). And that clear message is what matters, for it reveals the purpose of life. We exist for God. Every creature is made to worship God forever into eternity!

Sometimes, Christians will reach different conclusions as to what the text is saying (such as the identity of the beings around God in Revelation 4).

24   See also Psalm 119:23, 27, 48, 78, 97, 99, 148.

But we should never deduce that this is because the text is unclear. Rather, the lack of clarity lies in us, and not in God's revealed mind in Scripture! I am the one who is unclear. God is never unclear. That's why comprehending Scripture requires the best of our natural reading in supernatural dependence upon God.

How does this passage point to Jesus within the wider context? Don't settle for a generalized, superficial reading of a passage; dig deeply to find exactly what is being said, especially as it relates to Jesus. For example, in Revelation 5, we are introduced to the victorious Lion of the tribe of Judah (v. 5) who turns out to be a slain Lamb (v. 6) whom the four living creatures and twenty-four elders worship in the same way they worship God in chapter 4. Moreover, they worship the Lamb by singing a "new song" that focuses not on creation, but on the cross (vv. 9-12). So firstly, we learn that Jesus equally deserves our eternal worship, even though he is distinct from God our Creator. Secondly, we learn that the hymn of creation in 4:11 is now replaced by the anthem of the cross in 5:9-12. This implies that our focus as believers ought to be on Christ and his gospel, rather than on the prosperity of this creation—because we live on the edge of eternity.

Finally, are there any surprises in the text? This last question is my favourite! It's often where the gold is to be found. On my fridge is a well-known memory verse: "Jesus Christ is the same yesterday and today and forever" (Heb 13:8). It is quite clear: Jesus doesn't change. This is a gloriously comforting and magnificent truth. But why does this well-known verse appear here, at this point in the chapter? Hebrews 13 is full of commands that initially seem so randomly associated. Have a look at verses 7-9:

> [7] Remember your leaders, those who spoke to you the word of God. Consider the outcome of their way of life and imitate their faith. [8] Jesus Christ is the same yesterday and today and forever. [9] Do not be led away by diverse and strange teachings, for it is good for the heart to be strengthened by grace, not by foods, which have not benefited those devoted to them.

Here's the surprise: read verse 7, skip over verse 8, and just read straight on to verse 9. Our well-known memory verse appears to be surprisingly **unnecessary**! So how does the unchanging nature of Jesus add anything to the commands on either side? It's a great verse, but why is it here? Before reading on, why don't you read verses 7, 8 and 9 a few times again and search for the answer?

The treasure is in the text. The prior command is to remember your leaders. Why? Because they are the ones who spoke the word of God to you. They spoke the message of Jesus to you. And this message never changes! Jesus is the same yesterday, today and forever. Your leaders are transitory, but their message regarding Jesus is permanent. As such, consider the consistency of their teaching and their lives (v. 7)! Don't be led astray by those who teach a different message (v. 9). The leaders to be remembered are those who will never teach any different news regarding the grace of God in Jesus.[25] Unlike religiously motivated eating habits, faithful, Christ-centred teaching will strengthen our hearts.[26]

So mine the Bible for the treasures. It's full of gold.

These steps are very important as we prayerfully comprehend God's intended meaning instead of our own. But there's more…

---

25 Note Galatians 1:8-9.
26 I am indebted to Phillip Jensen for this insight from a sermon. See *A Service of Thanksgiving—Richard & Jeanette Chin,* Phillip Jensen website, 18 January 2020. phillipjensen.com/resources/a-service-of-thanksgiving-richard-jeanette-chin

5.

A TEXT WITHOUT A CONTEXT IS A CON

Words and phrases find their meaning in their context. While I am writing this book, in early 2021, university students in Australia use the word 'sick' to describe either a friend with a fever or a band whose music they like. The context determines the meaning. So a text *without a context* is a con!

When it comes to the Bible, we must observe the *literary* context.

The literary context considers how a verse fits within its chapter and book, and also within the whole Bible. It is quite different from the *historical* context, which explores how the historical situation of the original readers might impact the passage. While the historical context can aid us greatly, our historical knowledge is always incomplete, and should never overturn the plain meaning arising from the immediate literary context.

To read the Bible better, it helps to consider how words, phrases, ideas and characters from your passage are linked within the:

1. immediate context (how does the passage fit within the paragraph and chapter?)
2. book's context (how does the passage fit within the whole book?)
3. Bible's context (how does the passage fit within the overarching story and theology of Scripture?)

As you read the Bible, you will see how these three points interrelate and inform one another.

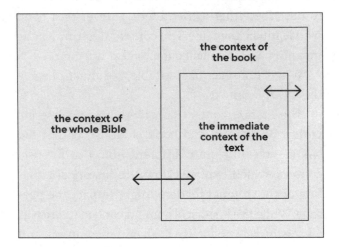

What follows is an example of how all three contexts apply to Ephesians 5.

1. The immediate context

In Ephesians 5, the apostle Paul commands the Ephesians that they should be "submitting to one another out of reverence for Christ" (v. 21). What does this mean? Does this mean that there is to be a reciprocal submission between husbands and wives, parents and children, bondservants and masters (5:22-6:9)? After all, Paul also says: "there is neither Jew nor Greek, there is neither slave nor free, there is no male and female, for you are all one in Christ Jesus" (Gal 3:28).[27] Furthermore, the historical context of the first century suggests that women were treated as inferior to men—but surely Paul wouldn't endorse such treatment.

Here's where we need to look carefully at the immediate literary context.

> [15] Look carefully then how you walk, not
> as unwise but as wise, [16] making the best

---

27   The immediate context of Galatians 3:28 has to do with being fellow heirs according to the promise of salvation. There is no difference among us as *heirs*. But there is a difference in how we relate to one another that demonstrates what it means to be filled with the Spirit (Eph 5:18-6:9).

use of the time, because the days are evil. [17] Therefore do not be foolish but understand what the will of the Lord is. [18] And do not get drunk with wine, for that is debauchery, but be filled with the Spirit, [19] addressing one another in psalms and hymns and spiritual songs, singing and making melody to the Lord with your heart, [20] giving thanks always and for everything to God the Father in the name of our Lord Jesus Christ, [21] submitting to one another out of reverence for Christ. (Eph 5:15-21)

The instructions around submission are an expression of a new "walk" (v. 15). It involves:

» wise living according to God's will during these 'days of evil' (v. 16)

» two primary commands: not getting drunk, and being filled with the Spirit (v. 18).

Submission, then, is one of five activities that express what it means to be "filled with the Spirit".

This is the flow of logic:

» Do not get drunk on wine, BUT instead (notice the contrasting conjunction!) be filled with the Spirit:

› *addressing* one another in psalms, hymns and spiritual songs

- › *singing*
- › *making melody* to the Lord with your heart
- › *giving thanks* to God always for everything
- › *submitting* to one another.

So the immediate context shows that **submitting to one another is one of five activities involved in being filled with the Spirit**. The subsequent verses (from 5:22-6:9) apply the specifics of submission *within various ordered relationships*—wives to husbands, children to parents, bondservants to masters.

The literary context is so important. Without it, we can easily make assumptions and miss God's good and intended meaning.

2. The book's context

Within the whole book of Ephesians, the command to submit to one another comes in the context of God's eternal plan, fulfilled in Christ, and worked out in the church. God's eternal plan for the fullness of time is to unite all things—things in heaven and on earth—in Christ (1:10). It involves creating good order where everyone will gladly submit to Christ as Lord, and uniting one new humanity out of two (Jews and Gentiles) through the reconciling work of Jesus Christ and his cross (2:15-16). There will be both an orderly vertical reconciliation (between us and God) and a horizontal reconciliation (between us and others). Moreover, this plan is to be made known to the cosmic powers in the heavenly places through the church (3:8-11), and the church is to manifest this order through the spirit-filled activity of "submitting to one another out of reverence for Christ" in various ordered relationships (5:21). Here is a beautiful image of how the church displays God's wisdom to the cosmos.

3. The context of the whole Bible

Submission, as it's applied within the marriage relationship, is further explained in 5:31-32. Paul quotes Genesis 2:24: "Therefore a man shall leave his father and his mother and hold fast to his wife, and they shall become one flesh." The wider biblical context is this understanding, grounded in creation, that the first human marriage was meant to be an unbreakable unity.

But Paul applies the beautiful union of marriage to the ultimate, eternal, unbreakable, marriage union between Christ and his church: "This mystery is profound, and I am saying that it refers to Christ and the church" (Eph 5:32). As we read

Paul's comments about submission, we see that he understands the goodness of submission in light of the whole Bible. From before the ages began, God always intended marriage to be a lived-out illustration of the gospel. The husband shows us Jesus by laying down his life for his wife, just as Christ did for his church, with steadfast selflessness and sacrifice. The wife demonstrates what it looks like for the church to submit to Jesus: instead of complaining and criticizing, she gladly follows her husband's servant headship so that everyone can see what it looks like to gladly submit our lives to Jesus.

Here is how marriage displays God's gospel to the world. Human marriages are only ever temporary, but what they point to is gloriously permanent and eternal.

Here is the splendour of understanding a text of Scripture within the immediate context of its chapter, the context of the book in which it appears, and ultimately in the context of the whole Bible. The reward is well worth the effort.

6.
LET SCRIPTURE INTERPRET SCRIPTURE

What I hope you've seen from the examples so far is that the best interpreter of Scripture is Scripture. If God is the ultimate author of the Bible, then the people through whom he writes will have a consistent message, no matter what the genre or testament.

So let's look at some examples of how Scripture interprets Scripture within the three different contexts we've observed: the immediate context, the context of a book, and the context of the whole Bible.

1. An example of Scripture interpreting Scripture in the *immediate context*

Romans 14:9 says, "For to this end Christ died and lived again, that he might be Lord both of the dead and of the living". Here Paul firstly states the *fact*—"Christ died and lived again". Then Paul provides the interpretation of this fact—"that he might be Lord both of the dead and of the living". No-one else could make that interpretation apart from God himself.

2. An example of Scripture interpreting Scripture in the *context of a book*

The key hinge verses of Paul's letter to the Colossians are 2:6-7: "Therefore, as you received Christ Jesus the Lord, so walk in him, rooted and built up in him and established in the faith, just as you were taught, abounding in thanksgiving." One might ask, what is "the faith" they are to be established in? Notice it is not "*your* faith", but "*the* faith [that] you were *taught*". As we make careful observations and look for repeated words or phrases (see chapter 4), we'll notice that this phrase appears elsewhere in the book: "if indeed you continue in *the faith*, stable and steadfast, not shifting from the hope of *the gospel* that you heard" (1:23). In other words, "the faith" refers to the gospel. So "the faith" that Paul wants the Colossians established in is the gospel that Epaphras taught them (1:5-7).

In this way, Scripture interprets Scripture in the context of its book.

3. Scripture interpreting Scripture in the context of the *whole Bible*

As we consider the biblical context, there are two other categories to consider: biblical theology and systematic theology.

i. Biblical theology[28]

Biblical theology refers to the storyline of the whole Bible. Genesis to Revelation is one progressive, unfolding revelation of God and his plans for the world, all of which climax in the person and work of Jesus Christ.

The Bible is like your favourite TV series. There are multiple, self-contained stories within each episode, but all the episodes connect into *one* big, overarching story. Likewise, the Bible has 66 episodes

28 Good introductions to biblical theology include: V Roberts, *God's Big Picture*, IVP, Downers Grove, 2009; G Goldsworthy, *According to Plan: The Unfolding Revelation of God in the Bible*, IVP, Nottingham, 2010; and M Lawrence, *Biblical Theology in the Life of the Church: A Guide for Ministry*, Crossway, Wheaton, 2010.

(i.e. the 66 books of the Bible), but they all connect into one big story that climaxes in the person and work of Jesus Christ.

This is another way of saying that the Bible was written by God, through people, to others, **about Jesus**, for us on the edge of eternity. The Bible is a one-way street to Jesus. This interpretative key is particularly essential to reading the Old Testament the way Jesus intended us to read it (Luke 24:44).

Good questions to ask of any Old Testament narrative include:

» What is the story so far?
» What happens in this episode?
» What do we learn about God and the way he does things?
» What do we learn about God and the way he does things *through Jesus*?

It is the last question that ensures we read the Old Testament the way Jesus intended us to read it. As an example, let's explore the story of Gideon in the book of Judges.

a. What is the story so far?

The book of Judges comes at a critical stage of God fulfilling his promises to Abraham (Genesis 12). God has rescued Israel out of Egypt in the exodus, and has now brought them to live in the promised land, just as he said he would.

b. What happens in this episode?

Throughout the book of Judges, the Israelites are stuck in a vicious cycle (see Judges 2):

» they forsake God by serving other gods
» God justly hands them over to their enemies
» as they suffer punishment, they cry out to God for help
» in compassion, the Lord raises up judges to save them.

So the story of Gideon fits within one of these cycles, spanning 100 verses over three chapters (Judges 6-8). After seven years of oppression from Midian, Israel cries out to God for help and God raises up Gideon to save them (6:1-13). But Gideon does not trust God's promise of victory and rebels by asking for signs of confirmation using a fleece (6:36-40). Nevertheless, God graciously responds to his rebellious requests.[29] He enables Gideon to conquer the Midianites by using outrageous tactics

---

29 Please note that Gideon asking God for a sign is descriptive; it is not a prescriptive method for seeking guidance from God. This was all the more the case for Gideon because seeking a sign was an expression of distrust. For more on the distinction between descriptive and prescriptive passages, see chapter 4.

(see chapters 7-8), even though he was the least person in the weakest clan (6:15) with an infinitely smaller army than Midian (7:1-8).

c. What do we learn about God and the way he does things?

God, not Gideon, is the hero. God, not Gideon, sovereignly saves Israel and deserves all the glory. God is keeping his promises to Abraham despite Israel's (and Gideon's) repeated rebellion against him.

d. What do we learn about God and the way he does things through Jesus?

Jesus, not you or I, is the hero. Jesus sovereignly saves us and deserves all the glory (e.g. Eph 2:8-9). We do nothing to save ourselves. We are repeatedly rebellious, like Gideon and the Israelites. But just as God raised up judges to save Israel from punishment, so too God raised Jesus to save the nations in fulfilment of his promises to Abraham.

ii. Systematic theology[30]

Systematic theology is to biblical theology what a carefully curated botanical garden is to a natural forest. Just as botanical gardens often gather and organize similar flora into categories for observation and study, so too systematic theology gathers and organizes what different parts of the Bible teach, and summarizes them into doctrines. Here's a list of typical doctrinal topics:

Revelation	God	Creation	Christ	Salvation	Church	Last things

When done well, systematic theology will bring out the connections between such doctrines and provide the indispensable framework for thinking about the Christian life. In short, studying doctrine should lead to the praise of God and the practice of godliness.[31]

So systematic theology helps us to read the Bible better. For example, how can we comprehend

30 Good introductions to systematic theology include: JI Packer, *Concise Theology: A Guide to Historic Christian Beliefs*, Tyndale House, Wheaton, 2001; JI Packer, *Knowing God*, Hodder & Stoughton, 2005; P Jensen, *At the Heart of the Universe*, IVP, Leicester, 2003; B Milne, *Know the Truth: A Handbook of Christian Belief*, IVP, Leicester, 1998; and W Grudem, *Systematic Theology: An Introduction to Biblical Doctrine*, IVP, Leicester, 1994.

31 Packer, *Concise Theology*, p. xii.

this verse: "a person is justified by works and *not by faith alone*" (Jas 2:24)? At first, it appears to directly contradict Ephesians 2:8-9: "By grace you have been saved through faith. And this is not your own doing; it is the gift of God."

Alongside careful exegesis, systematic theology is what helps us accurately comprehend James. When we collect passages about the doctrine of Salvation, it is clear that we are not saved by our works. The whole of Romans and Galatians testify to this; to teach otherwise is to teach a different gospel, which merits God's curse (Gal 1:8-9). Small wonder that, even for Martin Luther, James seemed to be an epistle of straw that had "nothing of the nature of the Gospel about it".[32]

But alongside careful exegesis, systematic theology pushes us to see that, because of their different contexts, James and Paul use the word 'faith' quite differently from one another. Remember, a text without a context is a con! As we look more closely, we can see that James refers to faith as simply *intellectual assent that **does not** lead to good works*, whereas Paul refers to faith as *trusting the promises of God in a way that **does** lead to good works*.

32 See P Pavao, *Not by Faith Alone: The Martin Luther Paradox*, Christian History for Everyman website, 2014. christian-history.org/ not-by-faith-alone.html

Good systematic theology will help us understand how Paul and James testify to the same doctrine. And, indeed, allowing Scripture to interpret Scripture in its immediate context reveals the very same truth:

> For by grace you have been saved through faith. And this is not your own doing; it is the gift of God, not a result of works, so that no one may boast. For we are his workmanship, created in Christ Jesus *for good works, which God prepared beforehand, that we should walk in them.* (Eph 2:8-10)

So better Bible reading comprehends a passage in its chapter and in its book, within the whole story of the Bible and in light of biblical doctrines. This is how Scripture interprets Scripture.

CONCLUSION:
THE JOY OF YOUR HEART

I hope you now see why reading the Bible better calls for the best of your natural reading in supernatural dependence upon God. Remember, *the Bible is ultimately written by God, through people, to others, about Jesus, for us on the edge of eternity*. But knowing this is not purely an exercise in gaining knowledge. Knowledge puffs up, but love builds up (1 Cor 8:1).

My prayer is that this little book will help you to love the Bible as **the joy of your heart**, just as you love God, your church, your family, your community, and people throughout the world for the eternal praise of Jesus, to the glory of God the Father.

As we conclude, let's hear these words of the psalmist. It may be tempting to skip over these words, but please read these verses prayerfully, with supernatural delight and trembling. May we cry out with the psalmist:

> Your word is a lamp to my feet
>> and a light to my path.
> I have sworn an oath and confirmed it,
>> to keep your righteous rules.
> I am severely afflicted;
>> give me life, O Lord, according to your word!
> Accept my freewill offerings of praise, O Lord,
>> and teach me your rules.
> I hold my life in my hand continually,
>> but I do not forget your law.
> The wicked have laid a snare for me,
>> but I do not stray from your precepts.
> Your testimonies are my heritage forever,
>> **for they are the joy of my heart.**
> I incline my heart to perform your statutes
>> forever, to the end. (Ps 119:105-112)

APPENDIX:
A WORD FOR THOSE PRIVILEGED TO TEACH OTHERS

Reading the Bible better isn't just about you; it's also about helping others to read and understand it better. When the time comes that you find yourself preparing to teach the Bible to others, there are many important factors to keep in mind. Vaughan Roberts writes:

> If the world is to be reached and the church is to be built up, it is vital that many with gifts of teaching and preaching are set apart to minister God's word and that they stick to that task and do not neglect it… Perhaps the church could do with a better bulletin, a

tidier garden or a bigger building; these are all valuable things to work at. But it cannot do without God's word. So those entrusted with the task of teaching that word must stick to it, even if that means disappointing congregation members who expect them to do a multitude of other jobs.[33]

If there is anyone who must read the Bible better, it is preachers and teachers of God's word; after all, they can lead and influence many people. It should be no surprise, therefore, that teachers will be judged more strictly (Jas 3:1). If you are ever teaching God's word to others, please take seriously this awesome responsibility that has been entrusted to you.

1. Practise what you preach

As examples to the flock, please be sure to practise what you preach. "Keep a close watch on yourself and on the teaching. Persist in this, for by so doing you will save both yourself and your hearers" (1 Tim 4:16). Richard Baxter put it like this: "Take heed to yourselves, lest your example contradict your doc-

---

33 V Roberts and T Thornborough (ed.), *Workers for the Harvest Field*, The Good Book Company, 2006, pp. 12-14.

trine… lest you unsay with your lives what you say with your tongues".[34] John Owen wrote similarly: "A man preacheth that sermon only well unto others which preacheth itself in his own soul".[35]

Dear preacher and teacher, please read your Bible better so that you will preach to your own soul as well as the souls of those in your care.

2. Work through the whole Bible expositionally

Congregations enjoy hearing talks on interesting topics that feel immediately relevant, such as singleness, marriage, suffering and contentment. Similarly, Bible study groups are likely to find topical studies very engaging. There is, of course, a very worthy place for topical, doctrinal and biographical teaching. But it can inadvertently prioritize personal preference.

For this reason, the lion's share of our teaching ministries must be expositional in order not to avoid uncomfortable texts, or texts about which we are simply ignorant. Through expository preaching and teaching, God sets the agenda. Particularly

---

34 R Baxter, *The Reformed Pastor*, ed. W Brown, Banner of Truth, 1974, pp. 53-64.
35 Owen, *Works*, vol. XVI, *The Church and the Bible*, 1968, p. 76.

when it comes to preaching, expository preaching is the kind that *exposes* the Bible by methodically teaching through the different books of the Bible verse by verse, chapter by chapter.

In this way, expository teaching will inevitably show people how to read the Bible better as you expose the text to them and *show* how to properly arrive at biblical conclusions.

It might be hard work at first, but expository preaching and teaching will speak pastorally to different circumstances...

...giving a rocket to the lukewarm in one passage, and sweet assurance to the tender conscience in another; requiring us to stand out as godly beacons of difference in one instance, and to give way in all-things-to-all-men flexibility in another; condemning the futility of works-based righteousness in one place, and the foolish presumption of faith-without-works in another.

This is why we must read all of the Bible and preach all of the Bible. It is also why preachers must work hard in their application of each text, showing how its truth applies to different circumstances, personalities and spiritual conditions.

I suspect some of our evangelical forebears—notably the Puritans—were rather better at this than we are today.[36]

So move on from the sweet, simple delights of topical teaching, and provide a solid diet of meaty expositions and Bible study. As you work through the Bible chapter by chapter, let God's superior agenda nourish us all in joy, so that we can continue journeying on this narrow road to glory.

---

36 Tony Payne, 'A Bible for all of life', *GoThereFor.com*, 6 March 2019 (gotherefor.com/offer.php?intid=19433). Another great resource to help you preach expository sermons is A Reid and T Patrick, *The Whole Counsel of God: Why and How to Preach the Entire Bible*, Crossway, 2020.

❀ matthiasmedia

Matthias Media is an evangelical publishing ministry that seeks to persuade all Christians of the truth of God's purposes in Jesus Christ as revealed in the Bible, and equip them with high-quality resources, so that by the work of the Holy Spirit they will:

- abandon their lives to the honour and service of Christ in daily holiness and decision-making
- pray constantly in Christ's name for the fruitfulness and growth of his gospel
- speak the Bible's life-changing word whenever and however they can—in the home, in the world and in the fellowship of his people.

Our wide range of resources includes Bible studies, books, training courses, tracts and children's material. To find out more, and to access samples and free downloads, visit our website:

www.matthiasmedia.com

How to buy our resources

1. Direct from us over the internet:
   - in the US: www.matthiasmedia.com
   - in Australia: www.matthiasmedia.com.au
2. Direct from us by phone: please visit our website for current phone contact information.
3. Through a range of outlets in various parts of the world. Visit **www.matthiasmedia.com/contact** for details about recommended retailers in your part of the world.
4. Trade enquiries can be addressed to:
   - in the US and Canada: sales@matthiasmedia.com
   - in Australia and the rest of the world: sales@matthiasmedia.com.au

Register at our website for our **free** regular email update to receive information about the latest new resources, **exclusive special offers**, and free articles to help you grow in your Christian life and ministry.

From Text to Teaching

David Jackman

Teaching people from the Bible is a weighty responsibility for anyone. You may be speaking from the pulpit, or at a men's or women's event, youth group, Christian camp or Bible study group—whatever the setting, preparation is key. If you're looking for some clear guidance for that preparation, this little book is for you.

David Jackman has spent decades training preachers all over the world—young and old, experienced and inexperienced—to correctly handle "the word of truth". He has now distilled the essence of his training ministry into written form.

This is a masterclass from one of the evangelical world's most trusted Bible teachers.

The Book of Books

Geoff Robson

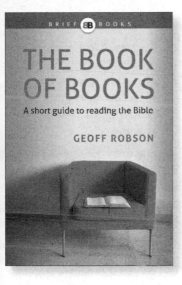

The Bible is an outstanding publishing success story, has had a profound impact on our culture, and many claim it has transformed their lives. The case to read it is compelling.

But it's a big book, written long ago, with words and ideas that may be unfamiliar to us. Where do you start? Can you trust that what you are reading is the original, uncompromised Bible? How do the different sections fit together and relate to each other?

This short introduction is for anyone—but especially for those who have never read the Bible before and who are not yet Christians.

FOR MORE INFORMATION OR TO ORDER CONTACT:

Matthias Media
mail: sales@matthiasmedia.com.au
www.matthiasmedia.com.au

Matthias Media (USA)
Email: sales@matthiasmedia.com
www.matthiasmedia.com

One-to-One Bible Reading

David Helm

Are there people in your life who you would like to see progress spiritually—perhaps a non-Christian colleague, a Christian friend at church, a family member?

Imagine there was some way that each of these people could grow in their knowledge of Jesus Christ. Imagine you could help them understand more of God in a way that was simple and personal—and that didn't rely on getting them to a church program or event.

All this is possible through one-to-one Bible reading.

In this warmly written book, David Helm explains the what, why and how of reading the Bible with another person, and provides plenty of ideas to help you get started.

FOR MORE INFORMATION OR TO ORDER CONTACT:

Matthias Media
Email: sales@matthiasmedia.com.au
www.matthiasmedia.com.au

Matthias Media (USA)
Email: sales@matthiasmedia.com
www.matthiasmedia.com